Pearl Jam

STAGE
FOR
SOUND

MIND YER HEED

Bass guitarist Jeff Ament wrote his own history of Pearl Jam...

Pearl Jam

To think all this started 7 years ago...

The Stone Faction

(Funny City Rock Guy with a Marshall)

Meets the Jeff faction

(serious Montana skate punk with a basketball)

Green River

3 records. 3 tours. The Seattle Sound sub pop Loud. Long hair.

Etc...

...mainly Etc.

One thing didn't lead to another and they left.

Mother Love Bone.

2 records. 1 tour... Love Rock. Lots of promise. Talk. Hype.

Then, Andy left to go do his solo record.

Once again, the Stone & Jeff Faction opt out 2 do a new thang.

Mookie Blaylock... Reeenk Roink...

Pearl Jam...

3 new guys. The Kiss ass function.

EDDIE...

(Master of words. Earth Guru).

DAVE...

(Percussive God. The quiet one... watch out).

MIKE...

(King of coffee driver guitar color, a blues man).

PEARL JAM...

Fate. Quickness. Hard work. No talk. No hype.

The coming together of 10.

...hands... eyes... ears...

with coitus & gold-E & a deep bench in N.Y. and L.A.

the journey begins.

like your favourite plant... just add water.

Watch Pearl Jam grow.

The real story, of course, was a little more complicated. It begins and ends in Seattle, the latest city to have the world's attention focused on its indigenous music scene. According to legend, it's the home of slackers, a city of grunge rockers, a bottomless seam of talent. It's the home of Pearl Jam, and their ancestors... Green River, Mother Love Bone, Temple Of The Dog. It's inspired philosophical reflection, media hype, even a note of hysteria and jealousy. And the entire concept of a Seattle sound baffles those who supposedly created it.

Ask Pearl Jam guitarist Stone Gossard: "People have called it grunge, but I don't know what that means. I can't relate to grunge." Or perhaps Kim Thayil, of Pearl Jam's friends and fellow Seattle rockers, Soundgarden: "Grunge is a really neat word. It was a good marketing term; it has a nice ring to it."

But what does it mean? Here's American rock pundit Grant Alden: "The 'Seattle Sound' is only vaguely about music. The shock, for the rest of the world, seems to be in discovering the rage of a generation expected to go gently into the good life...

waking up one quiet morning and hearing that anger spewing over the radio, the same disenfranchised wrath voiced in hard-core rap, the same fury that boiled over in the Rodney King riots, only voiced by underground musicians who come from different musical and ethnic traditions. Nirvana, Alice In Chains, Soundgarden, Pearl Jam, Mudhoney ...they've all risen from the shoals of a stagnating culture like some great unkempt beast. And, to their shock, they found that their alienation was broadly shared."

Maybe Mudhoney, hub of the Seattle rock scene in the late 80s, more central to any local 'scene' than anyone, including Nirvana, said it best. "Everybody loves our town," they sang. "That's why I'm thinking of leaving it. It's so overblown."

Escape the catch-all media retrospectives and Seattle looks different. What gave the town its unity was its geographical position...Marooned at the North-West of the United States, closer to Canada than rock centres like California; its climate, cold, wet and unwelcoming; its feeling of being outside not just the mainstream of American youth culture but on the very borderline of America itself. Writer Tom Robbins has wisely pointed out that Seattle and the State of Washington as a whole are located as far away from Washington DC (the seat of the US government and home of the FBI, CIA, military and all law enforcement agencies) as it is possible to get, and it therefore attracts the kind of people who prefer to live as far away as possible from such regulatory institutions.

The US rock business is still centred on the California/New York axis. Seattle grew up without considering that it could ever influence what happened on either coast. As soon as the initial wave of Seattle grunge bands conquered America, that naïve, carefree vibe was lost...

Mark Arm to make the switch from guitar to vocals. It was this line-up that issued the band's first solo record, on the Boston-based Homestead label, which thanks to its links with distributors Dutch East Trading Company, ensured that the 'Come On Down' mini-LP would be available in Britain as well as across America.

Green River rarely stood still for more than a few months, and the release of 'Come On Down' was quickly followed by the departure of Steve Turner, who jettisoned cult success for the chance to join the true inheritors to The Limp Richards' role as Seattle court jesters, The Thrown Ups. Later, of course, he reappeared in Love & Respect, before eventually regrouping with Mark Arm in Mudhoney.

His replacement was guitarist Bruce Fairweather, establishing the Green River line-up that would see them through another year or so of intermittent conflict and local success.

Every Seattle rock success story eventually lands in the same place: with Jonathan Poneman and Bruce Pavitt, co-organisers (not that organisation was their strong point) of Sub Pop, undoubtedly the most important and influential US record label of the 1980s. It started out as Pavitt's baby, first as a fanzine, then as a vehicle for compilation cassettes of local bands. There was an LP, 'Sub Pop 100', in 1986; then, a year later, an EP by Green River and a single by Soundgarden, followed by an immediate cash crisis. Enter Soundgarden's manager, Jon Poneman, with a wad of dollar bills: "We started the company on about $19,000. We spent it on space, a little bit of advertising, and on putting out those two records."

Their joint enthusiasm was contagious. "Jon Poneman and Bruce Pavitt were the first people that ever told me that this scene was going to be huge," Soundgarden's Chris Cornell recalled. And with their insistence on limited edition releases, coloured vinyls, and strict quality control, they soon refashioned Sub Pop from a tiny indie label into a cult.

Recorded in June 1986 but not issued until Pavitt had scraped the money together in July 1987, the five tracks on Green River's 'Dry As A Bone' EP epitomised the original, no-holds-barred, Seattle sound. Sub Pop made the most of their marketing skills. There was an initial run pressed with a begging-to-be-collected yellow insert, then another run with a pink insert, and so on. And as much as any album recorded between 'Deep Six' and Nirvana's 'Bleach', 'Dry As A Bone' alerted the outside world to what was happening in the most obscure corner of America.

The same month that 'Dry As A Bone' reached the shops, Green River began work on what was supposed to be an album. They cut a speedy version of David Bowie's 'Queen Bitch', and then set out on a batch of original material, all composed by the Gossard/Fairweather/Vincent collective, with lyrics added by Mark Arm.

By the time that the 'Rehab Doll' mini-album was completed early in 1988, the band had disintegrated. It was their ethos which sparked the final battle: as Mark Arm told it, "It was punk versus major-label deal". The band who, according to Bruce Pavitt, had "destroyed the morals of a generation", collapsed after a show at the Scream Club in Los Angeles. Arm wanted backstage passes for their friends; Jeff Ament had already offered them to record company A&R men, who didn't bother to turn up for the gig. Arm split, accusing Ament of putting cash first, principles a long way after. After that, the Green River ran dry.

'Rehab Doll' eventually surfaced in June 1988 as an obituary for the band; while various Sub Pop and C/Z retrospectives and compilations dragged together the fragments of the corpse one more time. With the death of Green River, we kiss goodbye to the elusive spirit of grunge: the path from 1987 to Pearl Jam in 1993 scarcely touches on the sound which is supposed to be the unified voice of Seattle.

After Green River, there was Mother Love Bone, which was anything but a continuation of the past. There were three survivors from the old band, Stone Gossard, Jeff Ament and Bruce Fairweather. With Alex Shumway electing to work in a movie theatre, Gary Gilmour (no relation to the notorious murderer, incidentally) took over the drumstool. *Plus ca change*, you might think, except that Mother Love Bone's vocalist was the irrepressible Andrew Wood, fresh from scandalising audiences in Malfunkshun.

Wood, by all accounts, was a legend in his own brief lifetime. An eclectic, daring lyricist, his unique vision twisted the sound of the band into his direction. Stone Gossard remembered: "Any word Andy liked, he'd work into a lyric in some strange way. He was a very amusing guy, constantly putting on a show. He's absolutely one of my favourite lyricists of all time. If he could have been anybody, he'd have loved to have been Freddie Mercury. But Andy was misunderstood in a lot of ways, and in the same way Mother Love Bone has been totally glamorised."

Wood might have emerged as the face of Seattle; but he died of a heroin overdose in March 1990,

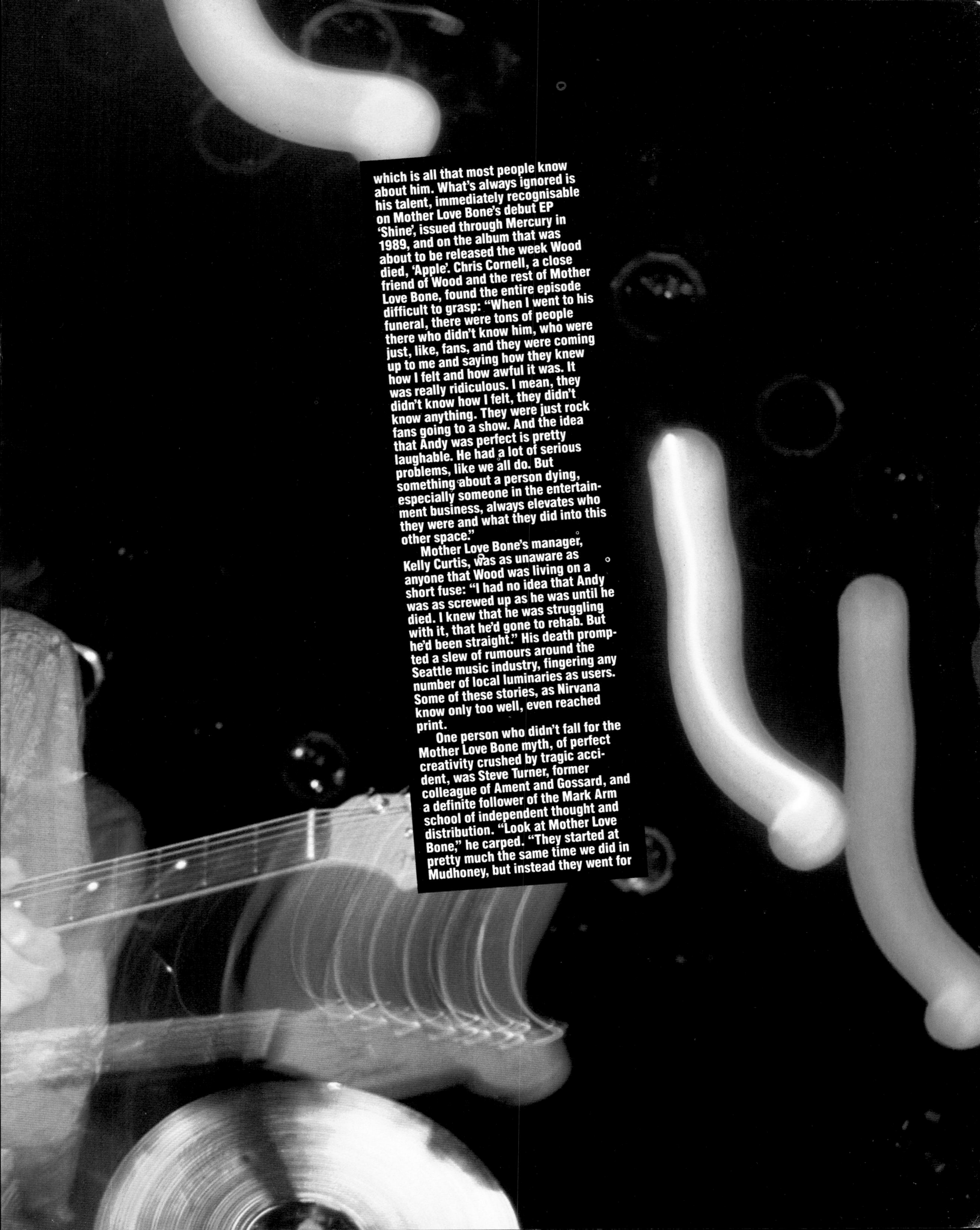

which is all that most people know about him. What's always ignored is his talent, immediately recognisable on Mother Love Bone's debut EP 'Shine', issued through Mercury in 1989, and on the album that was about to be released the week Wood died, 'Apple'. Chris Cornell, a close friend of Wood and the rest of Mother Love Bone, found the entire episode difficult to grasp: "When I went to his funeral, there were tons of people there who didn't know him, who were just, like, fans, and they were coming up to me and saying how they knew how I felt and how awful it was. It was really ridiculous. I mean, they didn't know how I felt, they didn't know anything. They were just rock fans going to a show. And the idea that Andy was perfect is pretty laughable. He had a lot of serious problems, like we all do. But something about a person dying, especially someone in the entertainment business, always elevates who they were and what they did into this other space."

Mother Love Bone's manager, Kelly Curtis, was as unaware as anyone that Wood was living on a short fuse: "I had no idea that Andy was as screwed up as he was until he died. I knew that he was struggling with it, that he'd gone to rehab. But he'd been straight." His death prompted a slew of rumours around the Seattle music industry, fingering any number of local luminaries as users. Some of these stories, as Nirvana know only too well, even reached print.

One person who didn't fall for the Mother Love Bone myth, of perfect creativity crushed by tragic accident, was Steve Turner, former colleague of Ament and Gossard, and a definite follower of the Mark Arm school of independent thought and distribution. "Look at Mother Love Bone," he carped. "They started at pretty much the same time we did in Mudhoney, but instead they went for

the major label golden carrot. A year later they had gotten a scrappy little EP out and were spending most of their time sitting at home talking to lawyers...and we'd already travelled around the world. A year after that, we had a few records out and had travelled around the world a couple more times. By that time, all they got to do was one scrappy promo tour and their singer was dead."

June 1990: Andrew Wood had been dead for three months, 'Apple' in the shops for two, and Polydor decided to drop the remaining members of Mother Love Bone. In any case, the group had already folded. That month, Soundgarden's Chris Cornell, who'd shared an apartment with Wood, wrote two songs about his friend: the elegaic 'Say Hello 2 Heaven', and the dream-vision, 'Reach Down'. Unwilling to lose the songs in Soundgarden's hard rock cauldron, he approached Jeff Ament

RECORDS
MILWAUKEE

By the spring of 1991, Ament, Vedder, Gossard, McCready and Krusen were ready to play live shows around Seattle. Managed by the same woman who'd handled Mother Love Bone, Kelly Curtis, they began sharing bills with another of her clients, metal merchants Alice In Chains. As the Seattle buzz began to grow, they attracted A&R men from the major labels. Epic won the toss, and by the late summer, the band were ready to cut an album.

First, they needed a name. Mookie Blaylock was cute, but an in-joke. They replaced it with another in-joke, but this one had resonance. Pearl Jam sounded impressive: what Epic didn't know was that it was taken from Vedder's grandmother, Pearl, and her finest recipe, a fear-some jam which supposedly had hallucinogenic qualities.

"Our first record was almost our sophomore record," Stone Gossard noted in 1992. "We had no time to make it at all." But it didn't show. 'Ten' (named, of course, after the number on Mookie Blaylock's shirt) was a staggeringly professional, inspired piece of work. Like 'Apple' and 'Temple Of The Dog' before it, it swept past any narrow preconcep-tions of the way Seattle grunge was

what could have been a vital publicity boost wasn't required by the time the movie was premièred.

In the States, the band had been out on the road with the Chili Peppers and Spinal Tap. Now, in February 1992, it was time to hit Europe. The album and single were held back to coincide with the tour, and Pearl Jam were introduced to Britain in Southend, and then at the Borderline, a breathe-in-and-you-might-squeeze-in showcase venue in central London.

Epic Records planned the show as an industry jaunt, and the crowd was dominated by label and press people. What they didn't expect were real fans, some drawn by the Nirvana hype, others by having discovered Mother Love Bone or 'Temple Of The Dog'. While insiders swaggered in, the fans were left in the cold. Horrified, Eddie Vedder and Dave Abbruzzese mingled outside, handing out free promo CDs and apologies. Despite that, the band still got the stick from reviewers who'd been allowed in for free. *Melody Maker* made one perceptive remark: their man reckoned Vedder was 'way too fragile' for the superstar circus.

Audience response in Scandinavia came close to terrifying the band; back in England at the end of the month, it was hatred rather than love that was the problem, when Eddie was catcalled by bigots for introducing 'Deep' as "a song about homosexuality". They ended their

debut tour at the University of London. Vedder diving deep into the audience, before the band dissipated their triumph with an aimless encore jam with their support act. Pencils were already being sharpened for the backlash.

No matter: 'Alive' topped the specialist metal charts, while 'Ten' was outsold only by the new LP by Love & Hate. A week later, though, the *NME* went in search of the new Nirvana, and found not Pearl Jam, but Pavement. Keith Cameron wrote: "Watch Pearl Jam and you see a bunch of raggle-taggle cool street guys equating sensitive with wanking their guitars. It jars something rotten, and it's hard to decide whether to feel contempt or pity." His attack stung Vedder into an angry response when the band returned in June. Pearl Jam's credibility wasn't helped when Kurt Cobain lent his considerable public weight to the controversy, denouncing Jam as "a corporate band", jumping on Nirvana's bandwagon. Jeff Ament maintained his cool, and simply reminded Cobain that before Nirvana, there had been Green River.

Meanwhile, the re-recorded 'Even Flow' was readied for release in April. That month, Pearl Jam headlined at the Limelight in New York,

encoring with Neil Young's 'Rockin' In The Free World' and The Beatles' 'I Got A Feeling'. And 'Ten' finally out-stripped 'Nevermind' in the US metal charts, *en route* to outselling that album worldwide over the whole of 1992. No wonder Kurt was miffed.

Two months later, the band were back in the UK, supporting The Cult 'In The Park'... London's Finsbury Park, to be exact. That was when Vedder let rip about the band's principles and passion, after being told about the *NME* story minutes before the show: "When I got on stage, I said, '*NME* says we're trying to steal your money. Don't buy the record, tape it off your friends. In fact, I hope there's bootleggers here who can make tapes and sell them. We want you to make money off this band. . . we don't give a fuck!"

Unfortunately, he did give a fuck, and the pressures were mounting on all sides. In June, the band prepared for a free concert in Seattle's Gas-works Park, designed to boost the 'Rock The Vote' campaign to persuade young people to register for the forthcoming presidential election. Three days before the show, Mayor Norm Rice pulled the plug. Eddie Vedder was distraught: "We knew we could easily deal with however many people turned up, but the Mayor and his people didn't agree. But it wasn't the *number* of people that bothered them, it was the *type* of people – 30,000 *young* people, 30,000 *alternative* people."

Back in Europe, there were some tempestuous shows in Scandinavia, before two dates in London. Pearl Jam never got that far. In Denmark, Vedder collapsed with what was described as chest cramps and exhaustion, though the official story denied that.

There were several problems. Vedder had been hassled by security men after stage diving in Roskilde; in Stockholm, the band's dressing-room had been raided, and he'd lost a note-book containing two years' of lyrics and stories. Mostly, it was their schedule: too tight and too tough. As Jeff Ament explained, "There were a couple of guys who felt that the whole thing was in danger of becom-ing not fun anymore. We called those shows off because we were in serious danger of burning out. The last couple of shows we played weren't as focused as we wanted. The vibe was totally angry and aggressive, not the vibe we usually have, and we felt it would be unfair to play for the fans that way."

MAGIC
WORTHY
MOOKIE
ABDUL
BIG O
EWING
ELGIN BAYLOR
RON HARPER
BOBBY DANDRIDGE

ALL AREAS
ALL AREAS

media profile, but the band is still very much a collective, as Mike McCready explained: "When it comes to writing, Stone tends to do a lot, but we all combine ideas. Jeff and I have written some stuff, and Eddie does all the lyrics." Stone added: "We all bring ideas in. I might arrange an interesting guitar part, but rarely does a song turn out how I first imagined it would, which is great. It becomes something totally different, but something totally cool too. That's the challenge of being in a real band: allowing everyone to have input, allowing the accomplishment not to be yours, but the band's.

"Writing a song as a group is a form of evolution. Some animals never evolve because they're so efficient at doing their feeding and mating routine; whereas human beings evolved so much more intently because of their brains. It has been easy for us to die off in great numbers when things fucked up, because there's constant turmoil. But turmoil is what helps us grow. It's an exciting part of being in a band."

And an exciting part of watching Pearl Jam stride and sometimes stumble through their first eighteen months of fame. The future, if nothing else, will be interesting.

ALL AREAS

A Pearl Jam Discography...

GREEN RIVER...

Come On Down (EP)
Come On Down/New God/Swallow My Pride/Ride Of Your Life/Corner Of My Eye/Tunnel Of Love
Homestead HMS 031 (12"), 1985

Together We'll Never/Ain't Nothing To Do
ICP 01 (7"), 1986

Dry As A Bone (EP)
This Town/PCC/Ozzie/Unwind/Baby Takes
Sub Pop SP 11 (12"), 1987

Rehab Doll (EP)
Forever Means/Rehab Doll/Swallow My Pride/Together We'll Never/Smilin' And Dyin'/Porkfist/Take A Dive/One More Stitch
Sub Pop SP 15 (12"), 1988

Dry As A Bone/Rehab Doll
Compilation of Dry As A Bone & Rehab Doll with bonus tracks: Searchin', Ain't Nothing To Do & Queen Bitch.
Sub Pop SPCD 72/239 (German CD), 1992

MOTHER LOVE BONE...

Shine
Thru Fade Away/Mindshaker Meltdown/Half Ass Monkey Boy/Chloe Dancer; Crown Of Thorns/Capricorn Sister
Stardog Records (EP), 1989

Apple
This Is Shangrila/Stardog Champion/Holy Roller/Bone China/Come Bite The Apple/Stargazer/Heartshine/Captain Hi-Top/Man Of The Golden Words/Capricorn Sister/Gentle Groove/Mr Danny Boy/Crown Of Thorns
Stardog Records (LP), 1990

Mother Love Bone
Compilation of Shine & Apple with bonus track: Lady Godiva Blues
Mercury 314 512 884-2 (2 CDs), 1992

TEMPLE OF THE DOG...

Temple Of The Dog
Say Hello To Heaven/Reach Down/Hunger Strike/Pushin' Forward Back/Call Me Dog/Times Of Trouble/Wooden Jesus/Your Saviour/Four Walled World/All Night Thing
A&M 395350 1 (LP), 1991

Hunger Strike/All Night Thing
A&M AM 0091 (7"), 1992

Hunger Strike/All Night Thing/Your Saviour
A&M AMY 0091 (12" & CD), 1992

PEARL JAM...

Ten
Once/Even Flow/Alive/Why Go/Black/Jeremy/Oceans/Porch/Garden/Deep/ Release/Master/Slave
Epic 4688841 1 (LP), 1992

Alive/Once
Epic 657572 7 (7" & cassette), 1992

Alive/Once/Wash
Epic 657572 6 (12" & CD), 1992

Even Flow/Oceans
Epic 657857 2 (7" & cassette), 1992

Even Flow/Oceans/Dirty Frank
Epic 657857 8 (12" & CD), 1992

Jeremy/Alive (live)
Epic 658258 7 (7" & cassette), 1992

Jeremy/Alive (live)/Footsteps
Epic 658258 6 (12"), 1992

Jeremy/Alive (live)/Yellow Ledbetter
Epic 658258 4 (CD), 1992

'Singles' Soundtrack
Compilation LP with two Pearl Jam tracks: Breathe & State Of Love And Trust
Epic 471438 1, 1992